DATE DUE

Paris Sketchbook

The Eiffel Tower from the Rue St. Dominique

RONALD SEARLE and KAYE WEBB

Paris Sketchbook

GEORGE BRAZILLER, INC.

New York   1958

For
Kate & John
who were left behind

MANY who see this book will know Paris better than we do. They will look for and probably not find, the particular places and things which symbolise for them this adorable city, where conversation seems wittier, steps are lighter, and hearts certainly warmer. But we believe that they will feel both relieved and complacent that we are ignorant of their special restaurant, their unexploited street, and we shall feel just as delighted if we learn that in here they discover an addition to their list for future visits.

We know that Paris has autobuses of enormous speed, danger and discomfort and that it has more, and funnier, policemen. We also had several encounters with the fiercer species of *concierge*, but we decided to jettison these quite familiar things to make room for the tragic sweethearts of the Porte de Vanves, and the exhausted animation of the ladies outside the Café de la Paix.

"Paris," Dr. Johnson once observed, "is indeed a place very different from the Hebrides." He then shattered this profundity by adding, "but it is to a hasty traveller not so fertile of novelty, nor affords so many opportunities of remark."

It is our happy task to prove him wrong. We think Paris is novel and remarkable. We also think it beautiful and stimulating. We believe the best way of proving this is to offer you drawings to look at. The text which accompanies them may be regarded as a faint prompting from the wings, a gentle murmur of conversation intended to keep you long enough before each picture to allow interest to awaken, memories to stir, and the charm of Paris in the springtime to sweep over you.

K. W.

Ronald Searle

Paris '56

12

THE FIRST HALF-HOUR in Paris is sometimes more painful than pleasant. Even veteran travellers suffer from the feeling that everyone is shouting at them because they are slow and stupid. They are torn between the fear of seeming ignorant, or being humiliated should they dispense the wrong-sized tip. But once the headlong plunge is taken there comes the first mounting excitement.

There, once more (or perhaps for the first time), is elegant white script painted on shop windows, telling of *vins blanc, rouge* and *rosé*; informing us that today *jambon* is 490 *frs. le demi-kilo*. Here is a *blanchisseuse*, her window a swirl of starry white dresses, pleated and frilled, and over the road is a small white bride on the arm of her beribboned brother, both stepping proudly towards their first communion.

It is at moments like this that we start delightedly exclaiming, "Oh, isn't it *French*!" and realise that from now on everything will seem like that. We are looking at Paris with the eyes of children arriving at the seaside, or of our own overseas visitors, gazing at Eros, and exclaiming at the public houses.

*　　*　　*

OUR FIRST NIGHT IN PARIS was spent in an over-large, expensive flat in the Place Vauban. Our first early morning view was of the gilded entrance to the Dôme des Invalides which houses Napoleon's Tomb, and we spent part of our first Sunday morning watching busloads of visitors pour into the great domed hall where he lay, "amongst the French people I have loved so well."

We guessed at their nationality by the way they came out. We fancied that the Emperor's countrymen walked with a graver, more reverent step. We were probably wrong. Finally, we followed a group of students as they came away. In their wake we trailed down the Boulevard des Invalides to the corner of the Rue de Varenne where, in the front garden of the Musée Rodin, we all halted silently before the familiar figure of *Le Penseur*.

The house was originally built for a rich wig-maker named Peyrence, who bankrupted himself giving wild parties. It was named Hôtel Biron after its next inhabitant, the Maréchal Biron. It afterwards housed a Russian Ambassador and finally a clutch of young nuns, before it became a museum. Rodin never lived there, but used for his studio the rather ugly little chapel attached to it, where the sound of his hammer must often have competed with the devotions of the nuns.

Neighbourhood mothers have long decided that the best part of the museum is its gardens, and here nursemaids come and sit while their charges play round the plinths of Adam and Eve. We noticed, while the drawing took shape, that the visitors to the statues were most often women, and were touched by an old lady who spent ten minutes gazing wistfully at *Le Baiser*.

*   *   *

OUR PARTY OF DEVOTED SIGHT-SEERS next led us down the Rue Saint-Dominique. We passed the Ministère de la Guerre, wondering what Napoleon would have thought of the net curtains at some of the windows, and finally arrived at the Chambre des Députés, also confusingly called the Palais Bourbon. Here, at the river entrance, we left them.

Napoleon's Tomb from the Place Vauban

Musée Rodin

Assemblée Nationale

Ronald settled his tiny stool on the paving stones of the Quai d'Orsay, where he looked rather like a disciple at the feet of Minerva. The most prominent notice on the front of this august building announced *Défense d'uriner* and I discovered, from the amiable *agent de police*, that the curved and spiked iron railings on this, and other corners, were aimed at preventing uninhibited Parisians from committing precisely this nuisance.

This brings us to the *vespasiennes*, which are inevitably among the first impressions any visitor has of Paris. Approval or disapproval depends chiefly on the visitor's sex. But there cannot be an Englishwoman exploring Paris who would not, at some time, have shelved her hygienic objections if only some such provision had been made for her. For the novice, may we suggest that you abandon any such hope and turn immediately into the most streamlined café within reach.

We found the elaborate but seedy example below near the Place Pigalle. Architecturally there are a number of different varieties, both in style, area of concealment, and (I am told) inside accommodation, but I was unable to narrow this down to more than a rough estimate that they are slightly more numerous and decorative on the Right Bank.

I also noted that in Paris lavatories are as conspicuous as letter boxes are concealed.

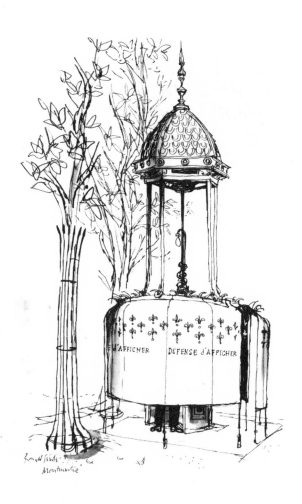

AS I WATCHED RONALD dodge in a frantic zigzag from one stream of traffic to another on his way to the island in the Place de la Concorde, I remembered the story of the herd of oxen who during the Revolution had balked at the stench of blood rising from the paving stones from nearly three thousand executions, and had refused to cross the great square.

Suddenly the sea of traffic rushing in from four separate directions, the scream of brakes and the wail of horns*, seemed like the howls of a mob watching their king ascend the guillotine. And the brief silence, following the bird-call of a policeman's whistle, was the shuddering moment when his head fell. The resumed noise was the yelling of the *tricoteuses* rushing forward to dip their clothing in his blood.

* Since the blowing of horns is now forbidden, Paris traffic continues at the same terrifying speed but in an equally sinister quiet.

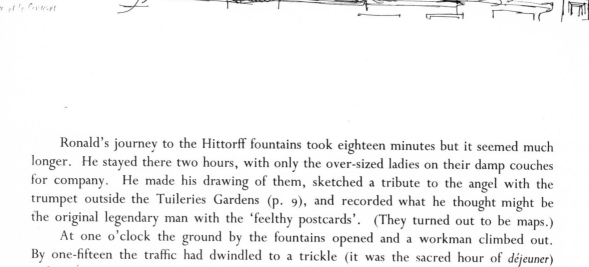

Ronald's journey to the Hittorff fountains took eighteen minutes but it seemed much longer. He stayed there two hours, with only the over-sized ladies on their damp couches for company. He made his drawing of them, sketched a tribute to the angel with the trumpet outside the Tuileries Gardens (p. 9), and recorded what he thought might be the original legendary man with the 'feelthy postcards'. (They turned out to be maps.)

At one o'clock the ground by the fountains opened and a workman climbed out. By one-fifteen the traffic had dwindled to a trickle (it was the sacred hour of *déjeuner*) and it was safe to return to the everyday world. . . .

WE IGNORED HISTORY for a day or two (as far as was possible in a city where every street embodied pages of it) and went in search of a place belonging entirely to the present day.

Some of our Parisian friends have reproached us for including the Sunday morning market at the Porte de Vanves. They say it is quite untypical, that the same poverty and squalor can be found in every big city in the world. But there was a Parisian quality about this couple, standing together in the rain. There was the good sense of their stance: face to face (we should have stood side by side and got our shoulders wet). There was a kind of gaiety in the careful arrangement of their wares, on a counter which was merely a piece of sacking spread out in the gutter.

They were offering for sale, like nearly a hundred colleagues, the few pitiful goods they had found, begged, or even bought. On this Sunday, they had seven articles to offer—a cup, a knife and fork, a key, a wheel, a door handle and a book.

Another 'stall' displayed one fountain pen without a top, two note-books and—a pair of white spats. But the owner backed away under the railway bridge and covered his face with a rag, when he saw we wanted a sketch of him. Some of the more prosperous-looking stalls had hundreds of items, and everywhere there were enough door handles, ash-trays, car mascots, wash taps, and nuts and bolts, to make one suspect the source of supply.

This is the poorest of the Paris markets. It is held on a vast piece of waste-land, at the extreme southern end of the 14th *arrondissement*, and in the neighbourhood live a number of coloured people, artists and beggars, all for the same reason—it is cheap. Inevitably, it is a Communist quarter and the scene of many political demonstrations.

Junk sellers. P^{te} de Vanves

The day of our visit brought drenching rain and few customers. But the vendors behind their soaked counters were ready to laugh when my newly-bought umbrella fell out of its handle, and to take trouble wrapping up some cheap glasses for which I had bargained. They took their standing-up luncheon of bread and salami as seriously as if it had been a *châteaubriant*. Indeed, one merchant refused to interrupt his meal to examine the ash-tray I was enquiring about, casually named a price of about three shillings and, when I gave it to him for wrapping, discovering that it was mother-of-pearl, did not retract. "*C'est ma faute, Madame, et vous avez de la chance.*"

sellers
te de Vanves flea market
28 May 1950

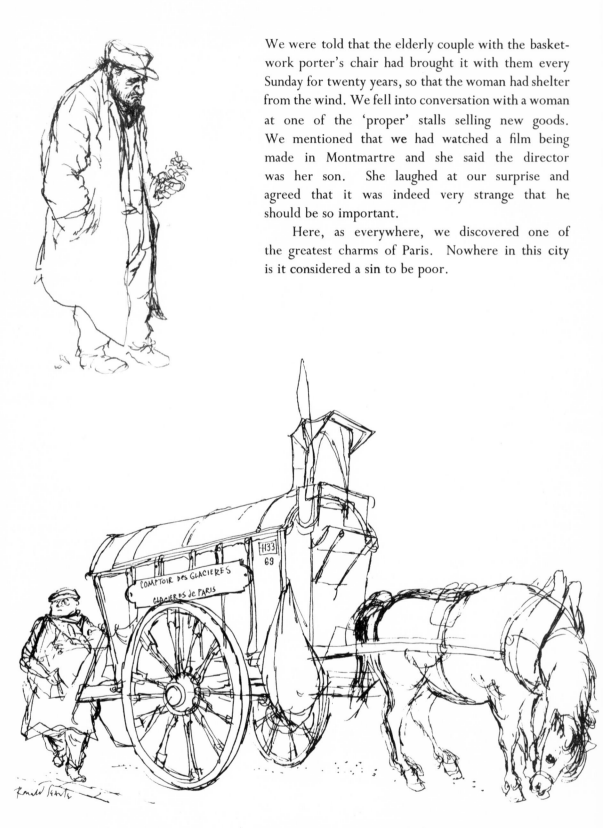

We were told that the elderly couple with the basket-work porter's chair had brought it with them every Sunday for twenty years, so that the woman had shelter from the wind. We fell into conversation with a woman at one of the 'proper' stalls selling new goods. We mentioned that we had watched a film being made in Montmartre and she said the director was her son. She laughed at our surprise and agreed that it was indeed very strange that he should be so important.

Here, as everywhere, we discovered one of the greatest charms of Paris. Nowhere in this city is it considered a sin to be poor.

THERE IS ALWAYS A FAIR somewhere in Paris. To find one on the doorstep of the
Gare des Invalides was to walk straight into the outward expression of the Parisians'
inward gaiety.

The one on the next page spread out on the Esplanade des Invalides, with the mouths
of the Batterie Triomphale (thirty-eight ancient cannon and four German guns) trained
straight on to the Dodgems, chiefly entertained Madame de Pompadour's downy young
legatees from the Ecole Militaire. On its outskirts, they bought paperweights with snow
drifting down on to a plaster Eiffel Tower (while the original rose amiably above them).
Here, they carried their girl friends on their arms ready to disengage for a salute when
officers appeared. But once gathered into the circle of music, blue flashes, rifle shots
and coloured lights, they grew bolder. Their favourite sideshow was *Les Nues* which
we noticed was the only one to stay open from morning till midnight.

When Ronald made this drawing, at ten o'clock one morning of our second week,
our favourite entertainment had left. It was a story-book engine, with a steam whistle,
a polished funnel, and a white-haired red-cheeked driver in blue overalls. This quarter
of Paris had not enough children; two weeks later we found him doing much better

business in Montmartre. But the rifles were still cracking (to hit a bull's-eye meant setting in motion a puppet guillotine execution), the lions were still roaring, although rather tiredly, and the little balloon-vendor was still looking as if he wished his wares would lift him off the gravel, and so ease the strain on his broken shoes.

Ronald Searle
Les Invalides

IT NOW SEEMS TIME we acknowledged those aspects of Paris which every visitor has somewhere at the back of his mind from the first moment he sees the lights go on in the boulevards or passes a butcher's shop and notices a *filet mignon*, set in a delicate frame of ivory fat, rolled to a perfect oval, and labelled *Je suis exquis*: we mean, of course, the food and the night life.

It is unnecessary to remark on French meals beyond a gentle reminder that they will take care of at least half of your cash total and will be worth it. Ronald drew a centre table crowned with baby lobsters, cheeses and wild strawberries, like a vivid still-life painting in the Restaurant Aux Gourmets, and once essayed to capture the sleek quality of my smile over the *café filtre*, but even he found no way of paying tribute to a cheese known as *le vrai Fontainebleau*, although his first encounter with this changed our dining habits for the rest of our stay. Afterwards no restaurant was visited unless this cheese was on its menu, and we spent far more time than I had expected in the Brasserie Lipp in the Boulevard St. Germain.

And we did not lay out a great deal of either our time or money in visiting the better-known and more obvious places. But of the endless stretch of cafés lining the Champs-Elysées we chose to record Fouquet's. Not only because it seemed to us to have the most character but because, it is said, Edith Piaf was discovered there one night as she sold violets and sang for *sous*.

The Champs Élysées at night, seen from Le Fouquets

Looking attractive and innocent by day, gay and slightly wicked after twilight, it is at once elegant and literary. Well-groomed women eat ices there in the afternoon, and at night-time *les vieux beaux* watch their gayer, gaudier, sisters making careful high-heeled promenades along the gravel paths. Street musicians play accordions or violins, flower-girls and sellers of children's toys pass between the tables. All along the avenue solitary figures are drawn towards the lighted café terraces to become other guests at this un-rehearsed and unending cabaret.

Tea-time at Le Rond Point des Champs Élysées

THE LIDO at the Arc de Triomphe end of the
Champs-Elysées was really worth the bottle of
champagne we had to order. It is one of the best
tourist entertainments, which is confirmed by the
number of Parisians who make a point of visiting it.

Like Moulin-Rouge and the Folies-Bergère
its high spot is girls, but it takes care to insinuate

at least two first-class acts between the *spectacles* and only the crooners are unintelligible to English-speaking visitors.

When we visited it the show contained Carrie Finnell, an outrageously funny comedienne, with startling control over her pectoral muscles. While she sang into the microphone, grasping it with both her hands, her bosoms beat a tattoo in perfect time to the military march and then independently cavorted while the audience roared with delight. The French papers informed us next day that they were insured for fifteen million francs.

Although in all Paris cabarets torsos are uncovered with monotonous ease, the bosom seems to remain almost unique in its attraction, and as a symbol of successful sex. Judging by advertisements and newspapers, pretty hair comes a poor second, and legs limp into third place. In Paris it is impossible to forget the feminine bosom. It is used in outsize posters for every entertainment where it is remotely possible. In any shopping street one window in ten displays the *soutien-gorge*; and every time we passed it there were crowds before a window which had dummy models wearing small circles with no visible means of support. The Paris Buff Book names four hundred manufacturers of the same article.

In most French cabarets the girls are in two groups—the strippers who lack in training and discipline what they make up for in loveliness, and the dancers. In the trained dancers' field, English girls are undoubtedly the most popular.

At the Lido and the Folies-Bergère there are permanent troupes known as The Bluebell Girls. Their trainer "Miss Bluebell" is herself an ex-member of the Folies-Bergère and some 1,500 dancers have passed through her hands. These girls work a seven-night week, from 10 p.m. till 2 a.m., and are not allowed stage door admirers. Indeed it is reported that after their performance they go home in a taxi—under escort.

Ronald Searle.

Quai d'Anjou 7 May.
Daumier lived in the last house.

IF EVER WE ARE FORTUNATE ENOUGH to have another long holiday in Paris, we shall make our home on the Ile St. Louis.

It is like a small sweet nut in the centre of a great juicy peach; an island in the middle of a city, with no *métro*, no buses and no taxi station, reached only by foot on one side and scarcely troubled by traffic from the Pont de la Tournelle on the other.

Along the Quai de Béthune fishermen lounge at the wide windows of the seventeenth-century houses, and call to the girls sauntering by the river below.

Even this tiny island was once in two parts; the Ile aux Vaches and the Ile de Notre-Dame. Its present name comes from saintly King Louis IX, who built La Sainte Chapelle which inspired our own King Henry II to commence his work at Westminster Abbey.

At No. 17 Quai d'Anjou the drainpipes, fashioned like dolphins (in black and gold), belong to the famous and beautiful Hôtel de Lauzun, in whose lovely rooms Gautier once worked and enjoyed his hashish dreams, and where Baudelaire lurked by day and left at night to gather his *fleurs du mal*.

At No. 9, which is marked by a pleasant wrought-iron street lamp, Daumier lived and worked (and *didn't* draw the sketches that are sold along the banks of the Seine).

Like a village street the Rue St.-Louis-en-l'Ile runs from one end of the island to the other, and its inhabitants have the

Mounted police

33

unhurried calm and friendliness of country folk. From the window of a *pâtisserie*, the golden horse outside the Boucherie Chevaline looked at us unreproachfully. Above his head a faded notice read *Ici on Achete Chevaux, Anes et Mulets*. Paris horsemeat shops are gay affairs in red and gold, and customers do not slip in furtively, as they do in London.

We were told a story about an elderly Russian countess who came to live in the city. She was praising the excellence of the shopping and particularly her butcher. "Such a nice man, such a clean shop, so gaily decorated, and as well as this his name has a Russian flavour—it is 'Chevaline'."

On the house next door is a plaque, recording that this is the Hôtel Chenizot where the Archbishop of Paris, who was wounded before a barricade in the Faubourg St. Antoine, was brought back to die on the 27 June, 1848. At the end of the street is the Hôtel Lambert, another famous and beautiful house, where Voltaire was once a guest.

Boucherie Chevaline on L'Ile Saint-Louis

THE HEART OF PARIS, and its birthplace, is the Ile de la Cité. Here, the first battles against invasion were fought, and from the square in front of Notre-Dame are still measured all the distances in France. On the Ile de la Cité stands the Palais de Justice, wearing the Sainte Chapelle like a jewel at its side and turning its formidable back on the shy charms of the seventeenth-century Place Dauphine.

Although it is only just fifty yards from the frantic bustle of the Pont Neuf, those who live in and about the Place Dauphine seem attuned to a slower, kindlier tempo. In the early spring morning, aproned girls and shirt-sleeved men slipped across the square to the bakery and strolled back under the trees, breaking off pieces of the warm bread to eat as they went.

A little later the artists took possession. A middle-aged man appeared, set up his easel with business-like celerity and worked in oils without pause until lunchtime. A girl, in red trousers and dark glasses, prowled for a time, finally settled her camp stool, and started operations with a box of crayons. Workmen idling under the trees examined the work of both, smiling but non-committal. The man ignored them, the girl produced a packet of Camels.

At lunchtime the place was busy with people coming to lunch at the delicious little Restaurant Paul, whose splendid food is only equalled by the friendliness of the waitresses. By three o'clock visitors to the Palais de Justice had turned it into a car park. Later it was invaded by tea parties, and in the evening it belonged to the lovers. Only in the early morning, empty except for a pair of silent dogs, did it seem exactly as it should.

Restaurant Paul

Place Dauphine

JUST AS EVERYONE exploring London must pass through Piccadilly Circus, so in Paris, every tourist is bound to cross the Pont Neuf, the oldest, longest and loveliest bridge in the city.

If visitors are rushing from monument to monument, the chances are that they will do no more than make a passing obeisance to Henri IV, eternally gazing from his horse into the Place Dauphine, his back to the Square du Vert-Galant where he once walked in the evenings with Gabrielle d'Estrées.

But if they pause to remember that this statue was made out of a melted-down Napoleon and a Republican General (in revenge for the first Henri IV statue which revolutionaries had turned into cannon), and if then a sudden rain-storm drives them to shelter under the bridge's piers, they will have the good fortune to discover another of the quiet green oases which turn up unexpectedly in all the noisiest parts of the city.

The Square du Vert-Galant is on the extreme point of the Ile de la Cité and we chose to imagine that the ancient poplar, which is at the foot of the steps below the centre of the bridge, was a sapling in the days when the King courted here. Perhaps it even witnessed his anguish in the days after his lovely, and loving, mistress had been poisoned in a nearby cherry orchard, and had died before he could reach her.

But when we made our annual pilgrimage to it last spring, it had gone. The custodian of the garden said it was condemned as dangerous and pointed out that there were other better, *straighter* trees serving the same purpose. As he pointed we watched a bareheaded young couple come swiftly down the steps. They went to the nearest tree, kissed each other briskly and ardently for a few minutes, and then in a business-like manner, walked back the way they had come. Yes, they served the same purpose but some of the poetry seemed to have gone—along with the dangers.

Through the spring and summer artists settle on the cobbles of the quay-side. They can even, like Ronald, go on working in a rain-storm, secure under the sheltering umbrellas of the chestnuts. And they share the silence with the fishermen who, tradition has it, are never seen making a catch.

Inside the little garden, children play quietly, while their mamas gossip. And the old, the wounded, the tolerated beggars, fidget and mutter or fall into uneasy sleep.

Across the water, by the Quai de Conti, tethered barges display lines of washing, small green rowing boats knock gently together as the big pleasure steamers go by, fallen pink chestnut flowers drift past and an occasional vigorous youth swims from one bank to the other and back again.

Ronald Searle

Pont Neuf

THE BOUQUINISTES HAVE gained stature in the three hundred years since their trestles lined the sides of the Pont Neuf, in company with junk dealers, quack doctors and all kinds of showmen.

When they were cleared away to make room for the increasing traffic on the bridge, they parted company with their mundane fellows and settled themselves, as a specialised group, on the parapets of the quays. Here they sold engravings, paintings and stamps, medals and curiosities, along with their books. As well as the bibliomaniacs, who were their natural customers, they attracted the custom of confiding young servant girls seeking a Romance to read or an interpretation of their dreams. And following in *their* wake came the young bloods anxious to supply both at first hand.

Anatole France, son of a bookseller, who claimed the *rive gauche* as his Alma Mater, wrote: '*Ye artless book vendors of the quays, my masters all. How greatly am I beholden to you. To you I owe as much, nay even more, than to school itself in the training of my intellect. It was you, good folk, who displayed to my enchanted gaze the mysterious tokens of a bygone age and all manner of previous memorials of the pilgrimage of the human mind. Even as I turned over the old tomes in your boxes and gazed within your dusty stalls laden with the sad relics of our sires and their golden thoughts, I became insensibly imbued with the most wholesome of philosophies.'*

In those days there were rare discoveries to be made. Now the *bouquinistes* know their goods only too well, and their *boîtes* rely chiefly on the patronage of tourists.

In sober moments only the most ingenuous expect to find bargains, but there is an atmosphere of hopefulness about the jocund water, the starry trees, the green boxes so full of promise, which disarms all but the most cynical, and obliges me to confess that on our first visit we invested a thousand francs in the purchase of two excellent drawings—signed with the name of Daumier.

THE FLOWER STALLS AND MARKETS of Paris are a reason for its gaiety.   No street can be drab when it is decorated with baskets full of tight red roses.   And can any woman resist a race whose delightful habit it is to present her with armfuls of flowers on every possible occasion?

The biggest and best flower market is to be found on the Ile de la Cité.   Here are avenues of freshly-cut country flowers alongside plants and flowering shrubs, strange-shaped yew trees and all the charming paraphernalia which goes with gardens.

The market spreads itself along the pavements of the Quai aux Fleurs, spills over into the Place Louis Lépine, and presses up against the walls of the Tribunal de Commerce. Florists, hotel-keepers and private buyers come hopefully up the steps of the Métro which deposits them amongst the stalls in the Place Louis Lépine, its wrought iron lamps and railings like sprouting sweet-peas, charmingly designed to match the market.

the Flower market
Quai aux Fleurs by Victor Hugo
May 6th 1950

Whilst Ronald was drawing this, I watched a gay, little Indo-Chinese lady, incongruously filming the potted plants. In her crimson socks, peacock robe and white shawl she looked an exquisite flower herself.

When the wind is favourable the perfumes from the market are wafted towards the Palais de Justice. They may even penetrate the grating of the prison where Marie Antoinette once waited for death. On Sundays the market also sings, for on that day the flower-sellers vanish, the stalls are hung with cages and it becomes Le Marché aux Oiseaux.

The fountain on the left of the drawing is one of a hundred similar ones known as Les Fontaines Wallace, which were presented to the city by Sir Richard Wallace (one of the founders of the Wallace Collection). Parisians often refer to him as an 'eccentric Englishman,' perhaps because he spent much of his great fortune on good works for the City where he spent most of his life. Only a few of these fountains are still to be seen. There is a lonely one in London, just off the City Road.

At the Bal Montagne

WE CAME UPON THE BAL MONTAGNE behind the Panthéon, the French Valhalla, perched on the Mont Sainte-Geneviève. Victor Hugo and Voltaire, who lie there, and Abelard, who lectured his students nearby, would have despaired to find such a place as the *Bal* flourishing in the centuries which they had dreamed would be so enlightened. But perhaps François Villon who grew up here, and was banished hence, would have chuckled.

The Bal Montagne is a dancing establishment not generally visited by tourists. Its most numerous clients appeared to be women who preferred to dance with each other. The band played perched on a platform against the ceiling, the cabaret was limited to a naïve dramatic recitation followed by a bawdy song and dance routine from a female impersonator.

The proprietress introduced the cabaret. An ex-actress, she has owned the *Bal* for twenty-one years, and has developed a ritual which the customers follow devotedly. The keynote was set by her opening announcement "*Mesdames, Messieurs—et les autres*" which, in response to pretended hisses, she finally amended to "*Mesdames, Messieurs et— mes amis.*"

In contrast to the sophistication of her establishment she seemed almost naïve in her pride over the décor; hundreds of coloured pictures of film stars cut out of magazines and pasted by herself and a friend all over the walls and ceilings. As the evening progressed Madame, who drank Coca-Cola "on the orders of my doctor", informed us that she adored *les arts, tous les arts,* that she rarely had trouble with her clients or the police and that her favourite film part had been as the bearded lady in *Les Enfants du Paradis*. Then she manœuvred us into her car and rushed us away to visit her "other little establishment", *L'Académie des Vins*.

This turned out to be a converted banana store, off the Rue de Rivoli, with gravelled floor, deliberately strewn with "dead men", lilies for decoration, waitresses wearing the silver tasting cup of the Wine Society, and a depraved little Bacchus, who bore some faint resemblance to his mistress.

Into this rather sombre atmosphere a busload of Danish tourists arrived. They were expected, for the young guide had previously looked in to check that they would be entertained and himself rewarded. On an instant the place sprang to life. A man played the piano, a young woman with a splendid voice sang "One Fine Day" and our hostess underwent a transformation. With her first words of greeting she became simple, unalarming, almost "jolly". No-one could have imagined her hurling insults at her '*amis*' in the Bal Montagne.

She started the whole company singing gay drinking songs, and told quite innocent funny stories which the interpreter translated. She then ventured on to some less innocent ones which he must have pruned in his translation, for she at once switched back to fun of a more straightforward kind.

In half an hour she had the originally stiff and slightly suspicious party blissfully kissing each other as forfeits and drinking a litre of wine without drawing breath. Even if the apparently spontaneous conviviality was laid on especially for them, and they were led to it like lambs to the slaughter, they went away happy, and this seemed to justify the deception.

As we parted (affectionately, for the wine was very good) Georgette Anys said to us, "*Faites-moi de la publicité, n'importe laquelle.*" *Madame est servie.*

Georgette Anys
at the Bal Montagne.

Ronald Searle

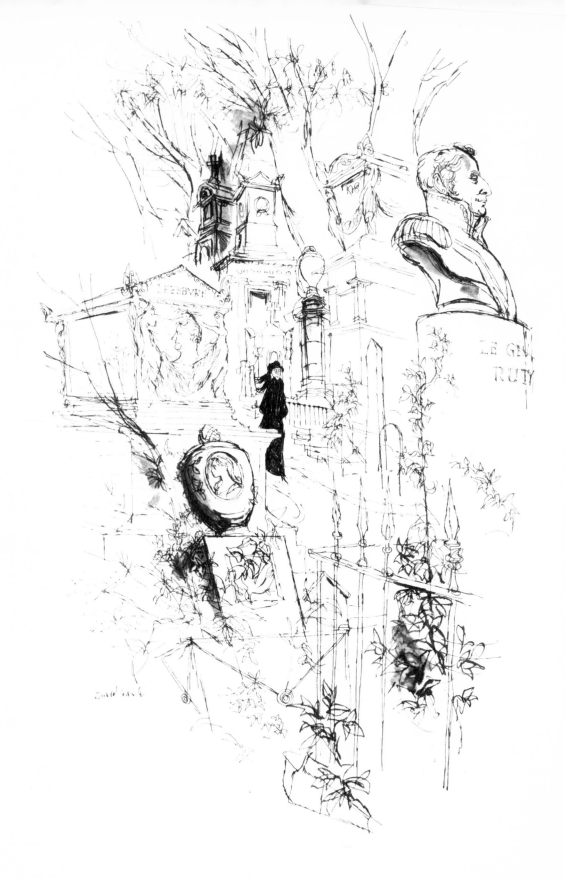

THEY CALL THE PERE-LACHAISE the *cimetière à l'anglaise* because it was conceived as a great garden for the dead. But it is much larger (109 acres) than anything we have in England and its monuments are severally grander, uglier, and more eccentric than our own.

Tombs of the illustrious to be found there include those of Héloise and Abelard, Molière, Delacroix, Sarah Bernhardt, Rachel, Proust, Balzac and Marshal Ney, but we paid our first visit to the one, sculptured by Epstein, which marks the grave of Oscar Wilde.

Commissioned by a Scots lady, sometime after his death, this had a lot of tedious attention from the French authorities. Epstein was charged heavy duty when he sent it from England and, before its official installation, the custodian of the cemetery who took exception to the uncovered figure had part of it smothered under a kilo of plaster. The artist and his friends protested so the whole memorial was covered with a heavy tarpaulin, (and curious visitors bribed keepers to let them peep underneath). After British and French men of letters had organised a protest, the cover was removed and a bronze plaque

fastened over the offending portion of the statue. Not long afterwards a gay literary gentleman appeared in the Café Anglais wearing the plaque round his neck. The tarpaulin was then replaced, and stayed until war ironed out such trifling arguments of officialdom.

We explored two others of Paris's twenty-three cemeteries—'in Paris there are more houses for the dead than for the living.' All of them abound with wreaths of flowers made of coloured china, which exceed even our own 'everlasting flowers' in ugliness and despondency.

In Montmartre, we found the Lady of the Camellias and, nearby, the tombstone of a trustful gentleman buried in 1867 which bore the legend *J'attends ma femme*. Alas, the space below was still vacant—she had never come!

'*ACCESS IS FREELY PERMITTED, so that you shall see some walks and retirements full of gallants and ladies; in others, melancholy friars; in others studious scholars; in others, jolly citizens, some sitting or lying on the grass, others running and jumping; some playing at bowls and ball; others dancing and singing; and all this without the least disturbance, by reason of the largeness of the place.*'

John Evelyn, writing in 1644, might have been walking through the Luxembourg Gardens with us this spring. He would have left out the dancing, unless he had chosen a *fête* day; but included children, sailing toy yachts hired for a shilling an hour, riding gay little roundabouts and swings, or shivering deliciously in front of their own puppet guignol.

He would have enjoyed the school of old gentlemen playing "*belote*" in the shade and been startled by endless avenues of statues, good, bad and indifferent, with which Paris is so fond of acknowledging her great, good and less good citizens.

"In Paris, at each street corner, is unfolded a page of history," said Goethe, reporting back to his countrymen. In the Luxembourg Gardens each avenue might well yield a ghost (if it weren't that every Parisian will tell you flatly that "in France we have no ghosts").

Walking past the ornamental Italian Gardens built by Marie de Médicis, we pictured Georges Sand swaggering ahead of us and disappearing with a last flick of her cane towards a wooded glade, which may

Luxembourg Gardens

53

have served Watteau as the inspiration for his Fêtes Galantes. These gardens have refreshed almost all the great Frenchmen of literature and art since the seventeenth century. Usually they came here at that time in their lives when they were as insignificant and uncertain as we felt walking in their giant shadows. Zola, Paul Verlaine, Baudelaire wandered here, and so through all the years, till the young American student, Jacob Epstein, came to rest between orgies of work.

As well as its big gardens, Paris is full of little parks, each with its sand pits, its swings and games for children. And in spite of the fact that it is so often surrounded by little iron railings, no one turns lovers off the grass.

It is said that one night the painter Degas and a companion stumbled against some of these railings. His friend cursed, demanded why they should be there at all. Explained Degas, "It is because they are afraid someone will come in the night and deposit another statue."

ONE DAY WE SET OUT to see and record the famous Place des Vosges in the Marais quarter of Paris. But when our taxi started hooting and chugging its way along the crowded and colourful Rue Saint-Antoine, architecture was temporarily abandoned and humanity triumphed.

Ronald huddled himself alongside the stall of an unfriendly ice-cream seller (ice-cream is the one French gastronomic failure) and I went in search of some information which would justify our change of plan.

Round the corner in the Rue de Sévigné I found the Musée Carnavalet, once the house where Madame de Sévigné lived, and wrote so many letters. It is now a granary of the city's relics, fascinatingly and lovingly displayed. Of all the Paris museums it is most worth a visit, although we guess you will find that the musket of a national guard fitted with an umbrella comes as a relief after rooms full of gory souvenirs of the Revolution.

Like the rest of the neighbourhood the Rue Saint-Antoine was part of the fashionable world less than a century ago. Now it is entirely working class, and a main thoroughfare from the Bastille to the Place de la Concorde.

On the right of the drawing, crowded in on either side by shops, is the Church of St.Paul—St.Louis. It was here that Cardinal Richelieu celebrated his first Mass, and Victor Hugo had his first child christened (afterwards donating two holy-water stoups). In a nearby cemetery Rabelais lies buried.

When I came back I found Ronald bewilderedly facing a gesticulating group of workmen and children. It seems that, for the sake of the composition, he had telescoped two shops together. They thought he had overlooked one of them and wanted to help him to put it right!

Wherever we had an audience, we found they would tell us with grave certainty that what he did was "*très bien.*" Noticing how frequently Parisians look over artists' shoulders without comment, we felt very cheered.

Rue Saint-Antoine and the Church of Saint-Paul, Saint-Louis

Ripolin

TRES VINS

St Paul's.

May 1950

THE NEXT DAY, risking no beguilements, we returned to the 3rd Arrondissement and wandered through a side street turning away from No. 1, rue de Rivoli. In the shadow of tall, crumbling houses, built without a thought for weary feet, we turned into the rue des Francs-Bourgeois and in a blaze of sunlight came upon the Place des Vosges.

Like so much else that is lovely in Paris, the Place des Vosges was built by Henri IV. Its grave arcaded beauty, the colour of faded terracotta, gently boxes in the gardens which were once a royal playground.

By the eighteenth century it had become a centre of fashion and no other square in Paris can claim association with so many celebrities of the period. We gazed at No. 6 where Victor Hugo lived for fifteen years—a fact that is still celebrated every year with a little *fête* by the writers of the district.

We followed a party of 'mamas' through a squeaking gate into the gardens and watched them settle into a tight little circle by the basin of the nearest fountain (a pattern repeated all over the gardens).

Under a chestnut tree slept an old man with a wooden leg heavily banded round with metal, oblivious of the children playing 'tag' around him. Oblivious too of the gentle old lady, apologetically collecting the 12 francs a chair demanded by the Sièges de la Ville.

And in the centre of it all, high on his marble pedestal, Louis XIII, magnificently riding to nowhere to the accompaniment of toy trumpets.

"I THINK EVERY WIFE has a right to insist on seeing Paris", wrote Sydney Smith to Lady Grey, in 1815.

There is little doubt that his sentiments are endorsed by the ladies who can be seen throughout the spring and summer ogling the shop windows in the Faubourg St. Honoré and sitting, exhausted but still animated, on the pavement outside the Café de la Paix. Their sensible English and American heads are all adorned with French hats which, on a swell of remembered gaiety, they will wear once in their native town before slipping into a hat box against the 'suitable occasion' which never comes.

The air circulating round the Place de l'Opéra is permanently sharp with the sound of English-speaking voices. The news-stand on the corner of the Boulevard des Capucines sells papers and magazines in almost every language but French and the girl who brings round the *pâtisserie* knows the day-to-day exchange rate for dollars and pounds.

Waiting for customers in the street outside are the *cabriolets*. The most popular of these had a woman on the box, wearing a black bowler hat and a hunting-pink coat. Her name is Rachel d'Orange; she is an ex-champion rider of

Café de la Paix

Europe, and speaks English well. We encountered her all over Paris pointing her riding crop at monuments, telling their story over her shoulder to her clients, who were seeing the sights in such picturesque, and expensive, comfort

Across the street from the Café de la Paix, ambushed behind a mass of statuary and secure in its own importance, is the Opéra, dimensionally the largest theatre in the world.

Here, on Friday nights, *les abonnés* (season ticket holders) come, wearing their tails and their tall hats which they are allowed to keep with them during the performance and wear in the foyer during the interval.

Directly underneath the Opéra flows the river Grange Batélière on its way to the Seine. Parisians are delighted to pass on the information that it first performs a certain office for the Folies-Bergère.

Not so very long ago it was actually forbidden to wear sports clothes anywhere in the Opéra. Our friend Bernard Grambert, as a student, was regularly stopped by the doorman and obliged to remove his pullover.

AN INFALLIBLE WAY of shedding strangeness, dumping inhibitions, of plunging into the swirl of life on the Left Bank, is to spend an evening sitting outside the Café Flore on the Boulevard St. Germain.

The Flore is no longer 'typically Parisian,' but it has the distinction of having sheltered Jean-Paul Sartre and his disciples, in the days when Existentialism was still just another exciting idea to be talked about over café tables.

Today its clientèle is a stimulating hotchpotch of young French, English and American students, of whom the Americans are the most enthusiastically French.

There are also left-wing journalists seeking copy and conversation; young publishers on the look-out for talent; tourists like ourselves, wanting entertainment; and occasionally a celebrity. It was here that we re-encountered Brassai, the artist-photographer who has done as much to immortalise the Paris scene as any contemporary painter, and who took us on some of our expeditions.

Sitting at the Flore we decided once again that Paris is the best city in the world in which to be poor. Here, for the price of a cup of coffee, a man may pass an evening in any type of company he pleases. If he sits for hours in front of an empty cup, warming himself, reading free newspapers while he waits for some friend who will certainly wander in, no waiter will flick him contemptuously away. They are more likely to refill his empty cup. In one famous café I have seen five young students sit for an hour or two

with nothing in front of them at all. Their waiter was so well-trained he would only come when they called him.

In the cold weather the Flore is a cavern of light and music. On a warm evening there isn't a chair empty on the pavement outside or a waiter standing still. The atmosphere is one of happy confusion, even the English voices at neighbouring tables lose their aggressiveness, become pleasantly blurred. And when an egg inexplicably flies into our midst and breaks over my own and my yoke-fellow's shoulder, we do no more than wipe it off in tolerant surprise.

NEXT TO THE FLORE is a small and *avant-garde* art gallery, La Hune. Next to that is the Café Deux Magots, whose literary history is longer and whose clientèle is almost imperceptibly more distinguished than its neighbour's. It is also perhaps slightly quieter, apart from Sundays, when the Flore is closed and the whole crowd moves two doors up.

There is a theory that the Deux Magots takes its name from the attendant baboons in Voltaire's *Candide*. It was already famous in 1899 when Oscar

Saint-Germain-des-Prés

Wilde would stroll up from his lodging in the Rue des Beaux-Arts to take his morning coffee. Gérard de Nerval must often have paused there on his morning walk through the quarter, perhaps leading his pet lobster on a length of blue ribbon. Years ago a favourite student sport was to go in and ask to see the proprietor. And when the unfortunate man came they would say—"No, not you, the other one."

The Deux Magots is on the corner of the Boulevard and the Place St.-Germain-des-Prés. Facing it, as serene and self-contained as the Café is sociable, is the oldest church in Paris, from which the quarter takes its name. It is also the loveliest and looks its best at twilight, which was one of the reasons we found ourselves back there so often as evening fell.

Place Furstenberg. Delacroix's Studio

All the streets round the Boulevard St. Germain hold memories of writers and poets. Number 6 rue de Furstenberg was Delacroix's studio, where perhaps he planned his lovely murals for the church of Saint Sulpice.

Now it is a small, little-known museum visited mainly by genuine art students; otherwise the square is given over to *concierges* walking their dogs.

Ronald, spending a blissful morning drawing without audience, and wondering about the unusual design of the street lamp, suddenly had his peace shattered by a fearful noise. A school nearby was having its mid-morning break and for ten minutes the *concierges*, with the manner of those performing a daily duty, drove small boys out of their yards, defended their dogs and muttered imprecations. A whistle blew and silence returned as quickly as it had vanished.

THERE ARE SEVERAL THOUSAND AMERICANS living on the Left Bank. Most of them are students and they tumble like infatuated ducklings into the life of cafés and clubs, where, perhaps because of their youthful experience in soda fountains, they take on local colour more quickly than their less numerous English contemporaries.

But they have also made big contributions to the life and atmosphere of the quarter. The Club St.-Germain-des-Prés, Rue St. Benoit, a temple of jazz, is one of them. Like almost all the student clubs it is known as a 'cave' because it is in a cellar. For the rent of a cellar is cheap, and there's no bother about noise.

The St.-Germain, like most of the other clubs, is small and hot. The dance floor is tiny and only two couples can perform wholeheartedly at the same time. From 10 at night until 2 or 3 in the morning it is jammed, with genuine members and sight-seeing tourists who have paid heavily for a temporary card.

The dancing is the main entertainment. On the evening we visited it, the 'stars' were a lively American girl wearing no make-up, and a tall, thin, collapsible negro. These two never talked to each other and rarely smiled. When they stopped dancing to wipe their wet faces, they immediately separated.

The method of taking possession of the floor was for a man, or girl, to start hopping and swaying on the edge in front of a fancied partner. Then, as soon as the couple in possession of the floor showed signs of flagging they grabbed each other and took over.

There seemed to be many more expert males of every age.

Club Saint-Germain-des-Prés

The night we were there only two young women, other than the 'star' turn, were asked to dance. The others lolled and watched sleepily.

The Club du Vieux Colombier, in the street of the same name, has been an unflinching favourite since it was first opened to cater for the young Existentialists. Today it advertises "Le Rock and Roll" but as recently as November, 1956, very few of its habitués seemed enthusiastic about this innovation. They cling to 'pure' jazz which is served up to them around midnight by an enormous negro. Bouncing every pound of his seventeen stone and streaming with perspiration, he sang brilliantly while a group of delirious female youngsters sat gazing up at him from the floor, wriggling and jerking with every beat.

The band was wonderful and so was his voice, but for the first and only time on our Paris trip we felt unresponsive. It was a relief, ten minutes later, to watch a shy ginger cat prancing silently amongst the shadows of the Palais-Royal.

THE FOLLOWERS OF JEAN-PAUL SARTRE
inherited some of his glamour as well as
his ideas. Besides its more serious effects on
thinking and behaviour, Existentialism in-
directly encouraged new forms of entertainment, and when his disciples started
running their own clubs, with songs and
sketches provided by, or reflecting, the
Master, elegant night-birds from the Right
Bank heard about them and started drifting
over for a bit of slumming.

They found these 'caves' wittier and
more amusing than their own rather con-
ventional amusements and their return visits
have turned the students' frolic into a
financial success, which has continued long
after the original cause for them had died.

Prices were quickly doubled, produc-
tion made slicker and some of the youthful
sponsors, 'cokes' in hand, huddled behind

Juliette Greco and Les Frères Jacques

the champagne buckets and were heard talking once more about "starting an entertainment just for themselves."

We visited La Rose Rouge, in the Rue de Rennes, during its first flush of fame, caused chiefly by the appearance of Juliette Greco, then a startling and talented girl in her teens, and Les Frères Jacques, four brilliant comedians, ready to take the world by storm. At 11 p.m. it was crowded and we used influence to get stools jammed between tables. Here we spent an agonising hour while a band, which I was frequently assured was excellent, split our ear drums. Ronald, tearing loose his left arm, sketched the décor and I collected driblets of conversation.

The most frequent subject, wherever I eavesdropped, was age, or rather youth; "*Elle n'a que dix-huit ans*" . . . the sex and the ages varied but the approval and interest were always there. Parisians really adore youth. They speak of it as if it were the supreme virtue. It is safe to say that any pleasant-looking child of seventeen can draw attention away from the most fabulous beauty of over thirty. She has *la beauté du diable*.

'*Le Petit Oiseau Noir Chante à Minuit*', said a Paris paper writing of Juliette Greco, whose clothes, fringe and unconventional behaviour (which included walking the boulevards in bare feet, and sitting on the kerb to rest) were faithfully copied by girls all over the quarter.

She opened the programme on the hour, appearing dramatically between the red velvet curtains wearing a black dress, with long black hair and unsmiling black eyes. She sang poems by Sartre and Jacques Prévert in an odd deep voice, infinitely stirring to the hearts of those under twenty-five and touchingly immature to the minds of those over thirty.

La Rose Rouge

Afterwards came Les Frères Jacques, clowning wildly as undertakers, policemen, and finally giving us a burlesque of a Western film which would have had us falling off our seats with laughter if we had not already been wedged together like figs in a box.

This year it was just as crowded, the 'stars' had embarked on their tour of the more brightly lit firmaments, but there was a very funny young man who seemed ready to follow them at any moment. *Plus ça change . . .*

JOUR & NUIT

BATTENDIER

La Stevia AU PIED DE COCHON La Stevia

AU PIED DE COCHON

La Stevia AU PIED DE COCHON La Stevia

Ronald Searle

Rue Lambuteau
Les Halles

near les Halles

ZOLA CALLED THE GREAT MARKET of Les Halles, pronounced lay-al (valuable information this, since it is the one place taxi-drivers cannot disentangle from the English accent) '*le Ventre de Paris.*' It operates in much the same fashion as Covent Garden, with Smithfield tacked on to one end. But it is larger, more orderly, and easier to penetrate.

At 2 o'clock one morning we explored the dark galleries. We passed neat mounds of cauliflowers, their white hearts looking like the upturned faces in a cinema; and trestle tables stacked with flowers whose colours pierced the gloom. Then, with dramatic suddenness, we came on a great lighted hall where men were cutting up carcasses. The dead animals hung in long rows, each one on its own hook, like children's shoe bags in a school cloakroom. In the centre of the hall, the delicate pink tint of the veal, the brilliant scarlet splashes of blood over the tiles and the white aprons, made it look like a huge-scale operating theatre, at once beautiful and shocking.

When the last cabaret is closed, and even the vitality of the Left Bank is ebbing, parties making a night of it take a taxi to Les Halles.

It is usual to finish up by eating enormous portions of onion soup and pigs' feet here, in company with the meat porters still wearing their bloody aprons. The uncertain, and the uninitiated, go to the large neon-lighted restaurants which cater specially for them, in price as well as *décor*. The knowledgeable choose to huddle into the tiny cafés, where the *pâté* of rabbit does indeed melt in the mouth, and genuine customers have learnt to tolerate their presence.

Towards morning the market grows more business-like. At dawn, buyers from houses and restaurants come to do their bargaining. By breakfast-time they are replaced by the smaller fry; the little *restaurateurs*, the enterprising housewives. These are followed by the tragic and the destitute. Beggars who turn over the sodden piles of refuse in search of scraps for soup. Crippled ex-servicemen offering bunches of faded parsley given to them in pity by the merchants. Hungry-looking women asking for five francs' worth of vegetables with which to make a meal. It was at this hour that I remembered that Les Halles stands where there was once a graveyard.

Meat Porter at Les Halles

PERHAPS I SHOULD REPEAT that this is a book of sketches. The subjects were decided by whatever Ronald felt he wanted to draw. My notes are personal, made at the time, and accompanied by whatever factual information I am unable to resist passing on.

When we met well-known personalities we were perplexed. We felt if we began to include famous people who were part of the Paris scene then we should have to pay our respects to all the notable writers, artistes, painters and politicians. We could not include Edith Piaf and ignore Maurice Chevalier, nor describe Marcel Aymé and not Jean Cocteau. As our time and our contacts were limited, and this was against the feeling of the rest of the book, we decided to leave all of them to the faithful attention of journalists and photographers.

However, we broke our rule once. It happened because our friend Bernard Grambert took us to the public performance of a radio programme called *Silence Antenne* which was written, produced and mainly performed by a pair of journalists, Robert Beauvais and Pierre Cour.

A surprise guest was announced and to everyone's

Fernandel
Paris. May 29 1950
Ronald Searle

delight, Fernandel, preceded by his fantastic jaw, his great teeth flashing, bounded on to the stage. He made us laugh, and like him so much, that we could not bear to leave him out.

Apart from his charming face, Fernandel's great advantage is that he was born in Marseilles. The Parisian regards a 'Marseillais' as we regard our Lancashire comedian. They enjoy the accent and think him a gay, amusing chap generally. Another accepted witticism has to do with the Parisian's pride in his military service. Instead of telling you his age, it is alleged he will say "I was of the *Classe* of '35", or whatever it might be. And no men love each other as much as two French strangers who discover they have served in the same year.

We found the cast of this radio show more casual and relaxed, and the audience less disciplined than ones we had attended in England.

Cacahuetes Grillées

IT WAS A GENTLE AND aged cartoonist, de Fleurac, known to his contemporaries as "*Le Président*," who suggested that we should visit the *Racing Club de Paris*. He said that there we should find smart Parisians relaxing in surroundings that were exclusive and "not at all tourist".

In spite of the Club's reputed 17,000 members, not suggestive of privacy, he was right. We admired the endless rows of tennis courts and the pleasant swimming pool, we also saw more pretty girls there than anywhere else, but for all its size and elegance the place had an English formality which, for us, made it rather uninteresting.

We were glad to get back into the green mysteries of the Bois de Boulogne, and listen to "*Le Président's*" memories of fighting there with his company of soldiers during the liberation of France, and of a duel fought at dawn less than fifty years ago.

The cafés and tea-shops in the square of the Trocadéro seemed to us to attract much the same type of clientèle as the Racing Club. Here too there was more elegance and evidence of wealth than we found in the more renowned boulevards. Here we actually *saw* a poodle wearing a wing collar, an embroidered coat with handkerchief pocket, and small rubber *bottines* to protect its feet from the wet pavement.

The peanut vendor hawked his sixpenny bags round the same four cafés during the whole of a drizzling afternoon. In spite of his blank face he had true salesman's technique. He would silently, and somehow affectionately, slip a nut or two into the hands of any children sitting at the tables, disappear and be within call again at precisely the moment when his small dupes were fretting for more. Even so he only earned about 300 francs.

FOR FIFTEEN HECTIC YEARS, between the two wars, Montparnasse was the centre of life on the Left Bank. Then, the Rotonde, the Coupole and the Dôme were the recognised headquarters of writers, artists and their models, and the various café personalities who, drawing the less spectacular in their wake, can make a place popular as soon as the coffee or the waiters please them. Just as abruptly and whimsically they will swarm, like bees, in some other place. Then more slowly, for first they must discover their deities' altered habits, the rest of their entourage will follow suit.

Just before 1939, these celebrities were beginning to visit the Flore in search of quiet, but it was the occupation of Paris that summarily ended the Montparnasse epoch, and when the liberation came, St.-Germain-des-Prés was in the ascendant.

The new locale had a good run, but by the time its fame had spread across the channel there had been another change. This year the Great Ones can be found in the little cafés further down the Boulevard St. Germain or sometimes in the Café Select of Montparnasse which, of all the old favourites, has resisted modernisation. Here I heard two knowledgeable-looking individuals murmuring that it seemed there was perhaps "the beginning of a revival".

Patrons of the Café Select

Certainly the big cafés, unfortunately now ablaze with neon lights and chromium plate, are busy after six o'clock and there is still plenty of 'atmosphere', for Montparnasse is the locale of most of the famous *ateliers*.

In the peak period of its glory, when tourists were buying pictures instead of painting them, and painters, used to being hard-up, suddenly found themselves with rich patrons and money to burn, Montparnasse was forever starting up new styles of cabarets and cafés, or holding riotous private parties and masquerades, often ending in a brawl and a visit to the night police court.

Some of the old places still survive. In the Rue de la Gaîté the Théâtre Bobino still has the best critical audience in Paris, and the Jockey Club has traces of the old sparkle.

But most of the *café-dancing* are sedate affairs springing to false life only when a likely-looking party of foreigners wanders in.

La Canne à Sucre has an upstairs bar and dancing underground, like most of its kind. We saw no food, but paid for our entertainment by the cost of our drinks—which the waiter indicated should have been champagne. The cabaret was a performance of Martinique songs and dances. Either male or female customers could dance with one of the three Martinique women, big, medium and little, who otherwise swayed endlessly round the room as if they found it impossible to keep still.

Kiki
deMontparnasse
May 195?

WE ARE LEAVING THIS DRAWING OF KIKI in our book, although today she is dead, because it may have been the last note of the most famous of all French models, and because she summoned up for us one of the nostalgic aspects of the old 'bohemian' Paris. When she lay dying, Foujita, the Japanese artist who had painted her in her youthful beauty, came to pay homage and say farewell to the Montparnasse she took with her.

In her life story, which has been published in English, with a foreword by Hemingway, she records that she was a "love baby, brought up with other love babies by my grandmother in Burgundy." Her real name was Alice Prin. When she was twelve years old her mother summoned her to Paris, where she earned her keep making soldiers' boots and selling flowers in the Rue Mouffetard. She also learned to rouge her lips with geranium petals!

At fourteen she worked in a baker's shop from dawn till midnight. One day the baker's wife scolded her for blacking her eyebrows with burnt matches and Kiki replied with her fists. She was turned out. She met a sculptor who asked her to pose for him.

Her mother was told, burst into the studio and finding Kiki in the nude, cried that she was no longer her daughter. Kiki had started her adult life.

It began in an atmosphere of squalor, immorality, and drug-taking. She later sold the journal *Montparnasse* in cafés, worked at book-binding and became a cabaret artiste. She was a delightful singer and might have become famous for this alone. But in the meantime, she had been discovered as a model and posed for Picasso, Derain, Kisling— and, of course, Modligliani,whose portraits of her now hang in many great collections of painting, and with whom she loved and quarrelled on a monumental scale all through the years when she was known as *La Reine de Montparnasse*. Much later she went to Hollywood but lost her chance because of her temper. She also had a sensationally successful exhibition of her own paintings.

She was fifty when we found her, in a brassy bar filled with noisy students and tourists. At that time she was making a nightly trip round such places, singing and dancing for odd francs, for as long as clients would give her a hearing, and sometimes after that.

She was stumbling about the floor, holding on to a chair to do an arabesque, clumsily throwing her skirt over her face to display her orange silk knickers, making play with the jazz handkerchiefs slotted through her garters. Her audience looked disgusted or pitying (depending on whether they had heard her story).

She preferred the treatment she got from the young students. When they started laughing at her, drowning her croaky voice, we saw a flicker of Kiki as she must have been. She stopped her song and swore at them in *argot*, viciously and with gusto, so that they subsided red-faced. Then passionately, and very much out of tune, she sang a traditional song of the streets, "*Les Mômes de la Cloche*," and silenced the room.

That evening she collected a hatful of twenty franc notes, smoothed them lovingly, gave a bunch to the pianist, and spent most of the rest to buy drinks for herself, the barman and any familiar face. When it seemed to be gone she wandered out into the night, to repeat her performance somewhere else.

Is it any wonder that we feel her ghost wandering reproachfully along the dark streets she once ruled. She was a great personality and a generous, loving woman.

Amédée

"ONCE," JEAN EFFEL TOLD US WISTFULLY, "there was a *chansonnier* designed like a *vespasienne*, but the police closed it."

La Tomate, in the Rue Notre Dame de Lorette, was currently the wittiest of this peculiarly Parisian type of entertainment. It was an intimate revue which only casually acknowledged the need for décor and costumes, concentrating on being satirical and often brutal about topical events and people. It is as popular today.

The *chansonnier* at La Tomate was Robert Rocca, and the high-spot of the evening was a patched-together film made up of news-reel shots of the French President which Rocca accompanied by his own verses with the refrain—"*le moyen Francais.*" While he sang how the ordinary Frenchman liked to "meet his friends, go out to dinner, take a little holiday, perhaps even ride in a motor car or sail in a boat" . . . we saw the President on state occasions, sitting at a banquet, riding in a great sedan car, boarding a yacht. . . .

There was also another film; amateur, silent, rather like an early Charlie Chaplin short, made by members of the company, and guying various laws and news items of the month.

The audience, who sat in the rather bare little room decorated with cartoons on the subject of the tomato ("*c'est bon et puis c'est nourrissant*"), by most of Paris's humorous artists, paid for their entertainment by ordering a minimum of 750 francs-worth of drink per head. They were mostly French and very responsive.

We should encourage the *chansonnier* in England. It would be a much healthier way of voicing our grouses than writing letters to the *Sunday Express* or slipping sly jokes into a T.V. act, and of course it is the perfect way of giving young talent a chance to try out new ideas.

It seemed to us that, in Paris, a man who is good at this topical lampooning is treated with as much affection and respect as a film star. We heard Raymond Souplex commentating on a Royal visit, the police strike and the quality of the new French Government. He had a corncrake voice, and so far as we could judge, his half-spoken, half-chanted verses were more remarkable for their wit than their rhythm, but he got rapt attention from a working-class aud- ience, who followed his every innuendo.

We had another splendid even- ing at the Club Fontaine des Quatre Saisons, chiefly because of the wit and charm of a tall worried-looking youth named Amédée whose anxious eyes won over the writing side of this book. His clowning and diction were so perfect that it seemed to us we understood every word he said!

Raymond Souplex

IT WAS BEHIND THE GARE MONTPARNASSE that we started our collection of graffiti. Plunging down a side street from the clamour of a street market in the Boulevard Edgar Quinet, we discovered, written in large letters on a wall so high above our heads that it seemed almost inaccessible, *Bernard Citroen n'est pas un mauvais poète.*

It was a gift from Freud. Here, we told each other, was the solution, the perfect way of explaining the difference between two countries. Where, we rejoiced, would you find in London someone taking the trouble to scale a wall to tell the world that someone else was not a bad poet? (Except, of course, the poet himself.)

We decided that from then on we would give all graffiti our earnest attention. What we discovered would turn out to be the key to the character of the district in which we found it.

It was a good idea, but it didn't work! Our next discovery, also in the Montparnasse area, was provocative but not particularly localised: *Coca Cola donne la douleur* it stated, voicing the resentment of those Frenchmen who hold that this particular aspect of American enterprise is spoiling the palates of the young, and incidentally, the profits of the vineyards. There was another to match it in a narrow alley-way near the Rue Jacob. Beneath a dozen tattered posters, advertising a Judo Club, was painted "U.S. GO HOME!" Underneath this was indignantly scrawled, in what we subsequently discovered to be lip-stick, *"AVEC TOUT NOTRE ARGENT??"*

After this our theory collapsed. In the neighbourhood of the Rue des Rosiers, we found *Amis, n'allez pas en Palestine, il n'y a personne à exploiter,* but no one can say that *Enlevez votre culotte* has anything to do with the highly respectable neighbourhood of the Avenue Raymond Poincaré.

The woman in the foreground of the market drawing over the page was selling mothballs. Her stall had a banner in huge letters crying "PARA-DICHLORDBENZENE." She stood silently smoking, her hands in her pockets, through an entire morning and only two nuns laden with fish stopped to make a purchase.

We saw her often after that; like a musty mascot she seemed to appear in every market we penetrated.

Bienvenue Market

Place Bienvenue – The Market
Montparnasse
21 Aug 27 50

WE SPENT A SUNDAY MORNING looking for treasure in the famous *Marché aux Puces* (more elegantly entitled by the stallholders *Marché Vernaison*) at Clignancourt in the 18th Arrondisement, and then stumbled into Chez Louisette, dusty, hungry and not very enthusiastic, for from outside it seemed just another restaurant.

As it turned out we stayed five hours. We were so delighted with it that lunch merged imperceptibly into tea, and tea into apéritifs. There was a young Dutch artist who sat near us all the afternoon, sketching the customers at two hundred francs a time, and a West Indian band which churned out *Le Troisième Homme* to order, but occasionally let themselves go on the drums and drew a hundred people to the doorway within five minutes.

Two young gipsies came in. They were wearing bright torn silk skirts and many beads. They silently offered to tell fortunes by putting their index fingers into their palms and raising their plucked eyebrows, but there were no takers. They draped themselves insolently by the great stove in the centre of the room, accepting Ronald's interest and his sketchbook as if it were part of their day's routine. When we offered to pay one of them to pose, she at once asked for double, but the rest of the room shouted her into silence as if she were a little animal.

Her name was Nina, she was twenty-one and her parents were Russian gipsies. Her mother 'was now in New York', where she had a 'good business reading the palms.' But, Nina said mysteriously, *she* wasn't allowed to go there. 'Not now or ever' could she have a passport.

She lived with a gipsy caravan which travelled between France and Spain. She had also been in England once, but did not like it, although the English were good at having their hands read, especially in Leicester Square. It was English soldiers who had taught her how to speak English (not very much and somewhat crude!)

Then she insisted on reading Ronald's hand. (It turned out to cost us five hundred francs.) She told him, obligingly, that this book would have a great success, and whispered her especial charm for his '*bonheur*'. At ten o'clock that night he was to put in his breast pocket a pinch of salt, a piece of bread, and a hair from his head. He was to keep this collection there, against his heart, for three days.

While she was with us I noticed that the young artist had a client. A man and black poodle were sitting opposite him; when he had finished the man took the sketch and invited criticism from other customers. The artist came over to us, looking defiant. "At first," he said, "I thought it was the man, but it was the dog . . ."

Chez Louisette has been owned by two generations of women. Today the proprietors are sisters who call each other Louisette, because it is a "*petit nom de famille.*" Their restaurant has become a favourite meeting place for artists and writers from all over Paris and the bar is always busy with stall holders from the market who have had a good day. The food is roughly served on paper cloths and there is hardly enough elbow-room in which to tackle the enormous bowls of *moules marinières* or the great tender steaks that one or other of the Louisettes will slap affectionately in front of you.

TWENTY-FIVE YEARS AGO, when M. René Bonnaire, who until his death last summer was one of the patriarchs of the market, first set up his stall in the *Marché aux Puces*, it was a trestle table standing on the bare earth. It had no roof, and every night he loaded his goods back on to a handcart and trundled them home with him.

In those days his customers were thrifty Parisians, prepared to make the long journey to Clignancourt for the sake of the treasures they would discover there. Today it is a commonplace expedition for tourists, and as famous as Petticoat Lane. Today, too, the stalls are more permanent affairs, standing on concrete bases, built over the years by

ALLEE
No 9

A corner in the flea market
Porte de Clignancourt

93

the merchants themselves.   Nowadays, they lock their goods into wooden shacks at night and leave a watchman and "*des chiens sauvages*" to guard them.

Some of the antique stalls are obviously more prosperous than others, and their prices seem almost as high as in Paris shops. Their customers pay a rent of between a thousand and four thousand francs a month, depending on whether they are old tenants or newcomers.

We noticed that the tourists tended to gather round the tables in the open. Where the goods were inside four walls they hesitated. They seemed fearful of being waylaid there and obliged to barter in a strange tongue, and when they *were* lured inside, they went with the bearing of people who know in advance they will come off second-best. For although here as everywhere the French sales people are courteous, and not at all persistent, they do have a disconcerting trick of making any kind of bargaining seem rather coarse and ill-mannered.

Clignancourt market is open on Saturdays, Sundays and Mondays.

The antique goods on sale mostly come from the buyers' market in the Rue Drouot, from private sellers, or they are sold from stall to stall. The merchants are resignedly aware that many of their customers are dealers with a better knowledge of values, and more ways of reaching rich customers.

It was midday by the time we found the antique quarter, having walked past hundreds of stalls peddling bright cheap clothing, bags, jewellery and ironmongery.   Our first "catch" was a huge, unshaven man sprawled fast asleep on an exquisite Louis Quatorze chair with spindly gilt legs.

Two stalls away a family was sitting in a windowless shop-front eating soup out of porcelain bowls at a magnificent carved table.   And in the next lane a little girl was doing her homework on a Sheraton bureau.   Ronald had no stool, so he perched on an empty trestle table opposite.   When he was halfway through, *Monsieur et Madame* appeared, unlocked their little store and silently started laying out their goods round his oblivious person without even suggesting that he should move.

It was ten minutes before he realised what was going on, and then they were most distressed that they had interrupted him.   They gave him a chair to sit on, insisted he place it exactly at the same angle, although this meant half their stall was shut off from prospective customers, and then left him courteously alone.

M. Bonnaire, who had the manners and bearing of a scholar, was once a confectioner. His was one of the less prosperous stalls, for although he didn't admit it, his wife privately told me they would sometimes pass the whole three days without selling anything. He knew something about painting and his weakness was buying unsigned oils in the hope of a great discovery, for he had once bought a Raphael with a pile of old pictures and sold it for canvas before he had had time to examine it properly. On that first Sunday meeting his proudest possession was the perfectly cured head and feathers of a tawny owl—"*Ça vous fera un joli chapeau*! . . .*"*

It wasn't just his noble beard which made us remember M. Bonnaire so clearly, it was that he had a courtliness and kindliness which made it a pleasure to be in his company.

M. René Bonnaire
at his stall in the Pce de Clignancourt
flea market

SIXTY GORY YEARS is something worth celebrating, especially when there is the problem of keeping the blood flowing regularly in the backstreets of Rue Pigalle.   Since 1896, in an alley off the Rue Chaptal, spine-chilling has been brought to a fine art and more changes have been rung on the horrors of the Boxer Rebellion than Dr. Fu Manchu could have dreamed of in a lifetime of opium taking.

At first glance, the Theatre du Grand Guignol would seem more suitably to house the Scottish Assembly than French Consuls, who misguidedly murder their virgin daughters to save them from a fate worse than death.   Even under the murky lamplight that set us stumbling over the cobbles, its cosy little gothic façade looked more inviting than many a building further along the street.   We brushed this aside, our anticipation too whetted to be put off by the outward appearance of things.   It was, no doubt, a subtle stroke of the management that the kindly old gentleman in an over-tight *smoking* who examined our tickets, should appear to be perfectly normal.   We shivered acknowledgement to the vampire we were aware lurked behind his off-white shirt front.   For was this not the birth-place of Grand Guignol, and has not, as our 100 franc programme put it, *l'adjectif* "*grand-guignolesque*" entered into the language universal?   Rather.

In wooden seats, reminiscent of the old-fashioned weighing machine operated by a retired seaman on Broadstairs seafront, we sat and gazed around us, whilst Beethoven's Fifth, slightly over-amplified, blew down our necks.   Not unlike a small baronial hall, panelled and beamed and papered with fading *fleur de lis*, the auditorium, holding at the most 300 victims, rapidly filled with cosy family groups. A damp current of air blew round our ankles—no doubt from the vaults beneath.   Behind the spyhole in the curtain we caught an occasional glimpse of an exceptionally beady eye.

The curtain rose on *La Dernière Torture*.   A drama in one act in which the action was passed in China, in the *environs* of 1900, during the revolt of countless *membres fanatiques* of secret religious societies.   The most ferocious of these sects being the Yi-Hu K'imen, better known as "The Boxers" . . .

The French Consul shot his daughter in the back, and our evening was nicely rounded-off with two acts of *L'Orgie dans Le Phare*. (Never was a lighthouse so orgy-ridden and never did a drunken lighthouse-man's girl friend burn so effectively as a warning to stray shipping.) We felt happy, as we made our way out into the night, that even in these days of Hi Fi and T.V., it is still possible to discover this outpost of the 1900's where twice daily on Saturdays a Frenchman can defy countless hordes of Yi-Hu K'imen with a walking stick.

GRAND GUIGNOL

THEATRE DU GRAND GUIGNOL

Ronald Searle '58

Théâtre de Grand Guignol
Rue Chaptal

Metro Barbès-Rochechouart

Rue de la Charbonnière

THE RUE DE LA CHARBONNIERE (Métro Barbès-Rochechouart) is one of the outposts of Montmartre. It is full of alarming "atmosphere", as if all the violence of North African nationalism were boiling inside its shabby, secretive houses. It seems to be chiefly inhabited by those Arabs who touted *les cigarettes Anglaises*, *American Camels*, *Chesterfields* . . . up and down the Boulevard de Clichy, during the days when the sale of any but French tobacco was forbidden in the shops, and who now wander rather listlessly about with carpets and peanuts and black-market *change*.

A huge, half-derelict hotel at a fork in the street is occupied mainly by Algerian workers from a neighbouring dye-works.

Ronald Searle
Montmartre
'American cigarettes, Joe?'

As we sat in an innocent-seeming café tasting *pastis*, the habitual Montmartre drink at ten in the morning, two villainous characters met at the doorway and silently exchanged a bundle wrapped in filthy rags for a wad of even dirtier thousand-franc notes.

Across the road, while wholesome-looking women queued at the corner for their bread, a huge Moroccan strode past them, carrying over his shoulder a kicking, screaming girl. He dumped her over the counter of a café and went away. No one even turned his head to look after him until, with a final shriek, she sagged to the floor. Then they dragged out a chair, lifted her on to it, and returned to their own affairs.

We had heard that some of the brothels had "gone underground" in this neighbourhood, or were converted into bars, with a convenient back-room. Certainly the three plump young women standing in the doorway of the Hôtel St. Ange seemed to confirm this, if not the name of their abode.

Ronald Searle

ONE OF THE DICTIONARY interpretations of the word 'ginguette' is 'tea garden,' but this one, on the Boulevard de Clichy, which is the beginning of tourist Montmartre, was offering more than scones and jam.

The notice board in front of the grille on the door read:

STOP! *Ici c'est Montmartre.* On Rit, *On Boit, On Chante.* On Parle Français, *Anglais et Argot.*

The entrance was one of the smallest we had ever seen. And the house was so narrow that we were horrified when we thought of the size of the room in which all this was going to happen.

The star of the establishment was announced as 'Claude Pierre, the queen of song.' We wondered if it could be the unfriendly-looking lady with the frizzled black hair gazing at us from an upstairs window.

We were passing by a gay-looking restaurant

called Aux Noyaux when we heard a faint glassy jingle and, looking up, saw a macabre ballet being danced above our heads.

The ceiling of the restaurant was hung with the empty shells of lobsters, prawns and crabs. Huge birds made of other shells were all jigging and bobbing as the wind drove the early morning dust along the Boulevard.

Down a side street we found a normal-looking pig complacently advertising a *charcuterie*.

Ronald set his stool up outside a shoe-maker's. He was unseated twice by croco-diles of sight-seeing schoolgirls being hurried rapidly up to the purer atmosphere of the Sacré-Cœur, and was finally scared away altogether by the two young women in the picture, who refused to believe that his inter-est lay entirely in the pig.

Palais-Royal from the Hôtel Beaujolais

Palais Royale. Paris
Aug 12 1952

WE DISCOVERED the true magic of the Palais-Royal almost too late. We had walked through its dim, lovely arcades and peered into the secret-seeming windows of its shops, which displayed precious objects of jade and porcelain, books, prints and model soldiers and endless stamps (this is the philatelists' Mecca), but never seemed to have customers.

We had gazed adoringly up at the windows behind which Colette, then still emphatically alive, was petting her cats and delighting her friends. Standing by the enclosed flower garden we had dutifully tried to reconstruct the fêtes and masquerades which had made this a riotous centre of the city's pleasures in the 18th century.

We sat with our feet on the rim of the ornamental basin, and shared the spring sunlight with the sparrows taking shower baths under the fountain. We tried to count the urns which pattern the balustrade of the houses rising so elegantly around us, and attracted the attention of a serious young student who told us that everything here was under the protection of the Beaux Arts, which undertook all repairs for fear of losing a little of Paris's history. He also told us that the notorious Philippe Egalité, duc d'Orléans, was responsible for its construction when, to raise money, he had gained permission from Louis XVI to build on to the gardens. He promptly made three new roads inside its boundaries, infuriating those nobles whose houses were cut off from the view, and allowing the merchants and their boutiques free access to the gardens.

Our student told us that, not many years after it was opened in 1787, Napoleon used to drink at the Café Corazza, and sometimes didn't pay, and that at a famous restaurant in the arcades a Prussian officer once de-
manded tea in "a vessel which has not served a Frenchman", and the waiter brought it to him "in a superb chamber-pot." And he mentioned, bashfully, that at night-time the first floor windows above the boutiques once glowed with rosy lights to display the charms of the ladies in residence there.

But it was an Englishman, generously entrusting us with the name of his favourite hotel, its bedrooms overlooking the gardens, who helped us to discover how to enjoy them properly. For to get the full flavour and charm of the Palais-Royal, you must observe it from above.

We moved there towards the end of our visit, and were made a present of Paris in miniature. We woke to an overture of splashing fountains and pigeons' wings as they came rustling and beating past our window, disturbed by the first morning visitors to the

gardens, dogs and their owners. We took our coffee and croissants leaning on the wide window-sill, watching the working-girls and men with dispatch cases, stepping briskly between the prim delicate rows of lime trees.

About ten, the first children appeared. They played sedate little games, the most ambitious being called, we gathered, a Serpentine; a human chain which was pulled, by a leader, rather purposelessly in and out of the trees, until weaker hands in the middle were parted. But the boys of ten played happily with younger girls and we heard and saw no bombs, pistols or sabres. It was all very reassuring.

Towards lunchtime, nurses and mothers gathered up the children and they were replaced by the students and artisans eating enormous *jambon* sandwiches, reading, talking in animated groups but, like the children, never noisily. It was as if the shadows of the past imposed a polite hush on their spirits. In the afternoon the children came back, and with them old men settled down to their newspapers and tourists hurried through with guide books, cameras, lighting meters and filters.

As the sun lengthened the shadows across the well-raked gravel, the morning workers reappeared, walking briskly in the other direction, and at six o'clock the dogs and their owners once more trod their self-absorbed measure. When darkness fell the gardens were closed, the shops shuttered, the pigeons restored to quiet, and the only life was the occasional clacking of anonymous footsteps down the grey stone galleries. And, high up, the lights shone from the windows of those fortunate residents who have this fascinating world under their hand and eye for every day of their lucky lives.

THE RUE DE BEAUJOLAIS is narrow and ancient and can be reached by car from one complicated direction, but more easily by either of two intriguing sets of steps leading down to it at each end. It was one of three much resented streets built soon after 1781 by Philippe Egalité and named after his three sons (the others are Rue de Montpensier and Rue de Valois). It encloses the gardens at the north side and originally contained seven or eight *Hôtels*, the Royal Hôtel Beaujolais being the last survivor of these.

Behind its unpretentious entrance at No. 15, you will find some of the authentic atmosphere of the *dix-huitième siècle* lovingly, though with difficulty, preserved. The exquisitely painted doors and carved ceilings on the first floor are a rare sight. Bedroom No. 9, once the end of the great saloon which ran the length of the street from No. 15 to the Théâtre du Palais-Royal, barely houses an enormous chimney-piece reaching to the gilded ceiling. It is dominated by a black marble bust of Lucullus which looms over-life-size at the end of the bed, so that you awake either startled and slightly disorientated or in a dream of glory, according to temperament.

In the first half of the nineteenth century the basement was given over to gaming rooms, and in the little gilded rooms above there was, as Madame Palletan will tell you crisply, "much licentious behaviour". It is to their credit that M. and Mme. Palletan have not been persuaded to modernise their hotel, which they have owned for fifteen years and which allows them no holiday. "We work, we sleep and we look at the gardens," but their reward is to have as their guests such distinguished men of letters as Giraudoux, Jacques Prévert and Albert Camus, who came here to write in peace, looking over the gardens. The visitors' book shows the names of Jean Marais, Foujita, Christian Berard, and Serge Lifar. But however great the men, all must climb the spiral staircase which leans outwards at such an angle that one must adopt a sailor's gait. And so must Germaine, who flies up after you with the heaviest of suitcases, refusing all help. But it is these things, the splendid morning coffee, and the calm unobtrusive friendliness of the owners, which make it now for us the only place in which to stay in Paris.

Next door to the hotel is the famous restaurant Vefour, not only one of the most expensive in Paris, but also boasting a proprietor who is able to bone a chicken in five minutes. In sad contrast to its luxury, the grating in the passage which ventilates its kitchens is a favourite sleeping place for many a *clochard* under cover of night.

Across the road, and remaining a source of amazement to all the inhabitants of the street who call it a "*véritable mine d'or*", is the Hi Fi Club, otherwise called Whisky à Gogo, with an ominously heavy padded door leading sharply down to a muffled basement. Here, every night, smart young Parisians press in to drink currently fashionable whisky at several hundred francs a glass and dance to a glorified juke box, into which they pour their own coins. Better value, it seemed to us, was Milord L'Arsouille at No. 5, a nightclub with a thoroughly French atmosphere, and a temperature of not over 90° Fahrenheit.

Hotel Beaujolais
rue de Beaujolais

WE THOUGHT A VISIT to the Place du Tertre (on La Butte Montmartre), the highest point in Paris, would be a good way to end our book. We knew that it experienced a charabanc invasion every afternoon, but we hadn't expected that Ronald would actually need to queue for a place from which to make his picture; or that there would be filming in one of the bistros, with agitated assistant directors darting about like rabbits, begging everyone to clear an area of three hundred yards and holding up cars travelling along the Rue Lepic. Or that, just as all was under control and the cameras rolling, there would be a major fuse and a small fire on the set! Altogether it was an exciting afternoon and just the kind of thing the tourists had come to see.

The evening that followed lived up to Montmartre's reputation too. Music, and noise, poured out of the twenty odd little bistros round the square. Sleek cars passed on their way to the restaurant owned by 'Lady' Patachou, which was once a little baker's shop and now has a hostess famous for cutting off her clients' ties if they don't sing her choruses. Then we came outside to watch the dancing in the square. In one of the bistros we learned to sing "*Quatre-vingts Chasseurs*," realising that as the verses continued the ice got thinner but

Place du Tertre

never hearing clearly enough to understand why.   Finally, standing beneath the icing sugar prettiness of the Sacré-Cœur, we watched Paris blazing away below us, and the Seine flashing with a thousand pin-points of fire.

This aspect of the Place du Tertre, the Bohemian one, is conscientiously preserved and displayed for its visitors.   But we came back early the next morning and discovered the other one—the quiet, self-contained life, so much like a village that the inhabitants talked about "going into Paris" as if it were a place quite remote from themselves.   And indeed, with no Métro beyond the Place Pigalle, and no buses to negotiate the steep incline of the Rue Lepic, a visit to or from the Place is in the nature of an expedition.

On this early morning visit we saw women, still in their *peignoirs*, comb in hand, sitting on little balconies and calling remarks to their passing neighbours.   Busy housewives slipped in and out of each other's doors, carrying steaming bowls of food.   Wild little cats darted across the narrow roads and played with the trailing branches of the vines. Somewhere in the distance there was the faintly plaintive music of the accordion . . .

It seemed to us that, as the sun rose and the striped umbrellas went up over the tables in the square and we noticed the faint mistiness in the air and heard the roar of traffic coming up from the city below, we were in a café by the sea. It was easier, now, to imagine painters like Renoir, Degas and Utrillo living and working here. The children looked very like the grubby little angels, with demon habits, who were made so famous by the artist Poulbot that they now have their own charity with its headquarters in the square.

We have heard people saying that Montmartre and the Place du Tertre were finished, were not in the least what they were. No more, they said, will splendid men have splendid thoughts here, or paint splendid pictures and get splendidly drunk afterwards.

We think they are wrong. In spite of the phoney painters and the greedy shop-keepers who live off its past glories, Montmartre is indestructible. But, unlike the rest of Paris, it is the first visit which will give most joy. It is a place for youth, and the trustfulness of the young which helps them to believe that all this delicious Bohemianism is a matter of the heart, and not the pocket.

Place du Tertre
Montmartre

Ronald Searle 1956

AND SO TO THE PICTURE with which we open and close this book: The Eiffel Tower seen, in one of its more modest aspects, from a café in the Rue St. Dominique.

When I was sixteen and on my first visit to Paris I stood under the great iron feet and pitied all men of delicacy forced to live in sight of its 50-mile grin.

"It's only *high*!" I remember saying, totally unimpressed by the "5,000 blue prints 15,000 parts and 2,500,000 rivets" which, my father told me, went to make up a marvel of engineering, and bitterly criticising the colour of the 37 tons of paint with which it is freshened every two years. Then this spring, as we came out of the Air Station, I realised with alarm that I was actually glad to see the thing. It was almost, as Ronald said, like the feeling we have when our train crosses over the Thames before it slows into Victoria Station. Mind you, we still don't admit that it is beautiful but, in spite of ourselves, it has become a symbol of Paris.

This reluctant tenderness seems to be shared by most Parisians. They all agree that it would be impossible to imagine Paris without it, which is quite a triumph for a building which has been standing only sixty-seven years, and for its creator, Gustave Eiffel, (whose heirs are still collecting their percentage of the lift fees, as well as profits on postcards, lead models and a very good restaurant on the first floor).

Probably no other public building has endured so many phases of popularity and abuse as La Tour Eiffel. When it was first built, for the Exhibition of 1889, it was generally reviled. "Monstrous, grotesque, dramatic, . . . of all the things Paris has made, it alone has neither wit nor soul" said Hilaire Belloc in 1900. On a visit to Paris in the same year, William Morris was once lost for several hours. He was eventually 'run to air' sitting moodily on the top of the Tower. He explained to astonished friends that it was the only place from which he "couldn't see the damned thing."

However, by the time the twenty years of life originally granted it were over, Parisians found that after all they didn't want to lose their bugbear. And besides it was a great tourist attraction. A little while after this a handful of "moderns" discovered that it actually *was* beautiful. Jean Cocteau made a film round it. Several people wrote poems about it. For a time the Eiffel Tower had glamour! But the wheel is turning again. During our stay a student was arrested hovering in its shadow and hugging a parcel of explosives. He explained that it was his philosophy to destroy ugliness, and he was going to rid Paris of a monster.

This drawing was not the first, or the last, in Ronald's sketchbook. But on the evening we left, we had a final *café filtre* at the table where he had sat to make it, looked fondly up the street and admitted how glad we were that 'it' would still be there, its thousand feet swaying slightly with the wind, ready to welcome us on our next visit.

Index

Abélard, 47
L'Académie des Vins (club), 48
Amédée, 86
Anys, Georgette, 48
Archbishop of Paris, 34
Aux Noyaux (restaurant), 102
Avenue Raymond Poincaré, 87
Aymé, Marcel, 76

Bal Montagne, the, 47, 48
Balzac, 51
Batterie Triomphale, the, 23
Baudelaire, 54
Beauvais, Robert, 76
Belloc, Hilaire, 114
Bérard, Christian, 108
Bernhardt, Sarah, 51
Bluebell Girls, the, 30
Boucherie Chevaline, 34
Bois de Boulogne, the, 79
Bonnaire, René, 92, 95
Boulevard de Clichy, 99
Boulevard des Capucines, 59
Boulevard des Invalides, 14
Boulevard St. Germain, 26, 63, 66, 80
'Bouquinistes, les', 42
Brassai, 63
Brasserie Lipp (restaurant), 26

Cabriolets, 59
Café Anglais, 52

Café Corazza, 106
Café de Flore, 63, 80
Café de la Paix, 59
Café des Deux Magots, 64
Café Select, 80
Camus, Albert, 108
Candide, 64
'Caves, les', 70
Chambre des Députés, 14
Champs-Elysées, 26, 29
Chevalier, Maurice, 76
Chez Louisette (restaurant), 90
Cimetière à l'anglaise, the, 51
Clignancourt, 90, 92
Clignancourt market, 94
Club du Vieux Colombier, 68
Club Fontaine des Quatre Saisons, 86
Club St.-Germain-des-Prés, 67
Cocteau, Jean, 75, 114
Colette, 106
Coupole, the (café), 80
Cour, Pierre, 76

Daumier, 33, 43
Degas, 54
Delacroix, 51, 66
Derain, 84
Dôme, the café, 80
Dôme des Invalides, 14

Effel, Jean, 85

Eiffel Tower, 114
Epstein, Jacob, 51, 54
Esplanade des Invalides, 23
Evelyn, John, 53
Exhibition of 1889, 114
Existentialism, 63, 70

Faubourg St. Antoine, 34
Faubourg St. Honoré, 59
Fernandel, 77
Finnell, Carrie (at the Lido), 30
de Fleurac, 79
Folies-Bergère, the, 29, 30, 61
Fontaines Wallace, les, 45
Foujita, 83, 108
Fouquet's (restaurant), 26
France, Anatole, 42

Gare des Invalides, 23
Gare Montparnasse, 87
Giraudoux, 108
Goethe, 53
Grange Batelière, river, 61
Gréco, Juliette, 71

Héloïse and Abélard, 51
Hemingway, Ernest, 83
Henry IV, 39, 58
Hi Fi Club, 108
Hittorf Fountains, 19
Hôtel Chenizot, 34
Hôtel de Lauzun, 33
Hôtel Lambert, 34
Hôtel St. Ange, 100
Hugo, Victor, 47, 55, 58
Hune, La (art gallery), 64

Ile aux Vaches, 33
Ile de la Cité, 36, 39, 44

Ile de Notre-Dame, 33
Ile St. Louis, 33
Italian Gardens, the, 53

Jockey Club, the, 81

Kiki, 83
Kisling, 84

La Canne à Sucre (club), 82
La Dernière Torture, 96
La Ginguette (club), 101
La Rose Rouge (club), 71
La Sainte Chapelle, 33, 36
La Tomate (club), 85
Le Baiser, 14
Le Penseur, 14
Les Enfants du Paradis, 48
Les Halles, 75
Lido, the (club), 29, 30
Lifar, Serge, 108
L'Orgie dans le Phare, 96
Louis IX, 33
Louis XIII, 58
Luxembourg Gardens, 53

Marché aux oiseaux, le, 45
Marché aux Puces, le, 90, 92
Marais, Jean, 108
Marie Antoinette, 45
de Medicis, Marie, 53
Milord L'Arsouille (club), 108
Ministère de la Guerre, 14
Modigliani, 84
Molière, 51
Montmartre, 22, 24, 52, 99, 112
Montparnasse, 80, 81
Montparnasse (journal), 84
Mont Sainte-Geneviève, 47

Morris, William, 114
Moulin-Rouge, the (club), 29
Musée Carnavalet, 55
Musée Rodin, 14

Napoleon's Tomb, 14
de Nerval, Gérard, 65
Ney, Marshal, 51
Nina, 91
Notre-Dame, 36

Opéra, the, 61
d'Orange, Rachel, 61

Palais Bourbon, 14
Palais de la Justice, 36, 45
Palais-Royal, 66, 106
Palletan, M. and Mme., 108
Panthéon, the, 47
Paris Buff Book, the, 30
Patachou, 110
Père-Lachaise, the, 51
Piaf, Edith, 26, 76
Picasso, Pablo, 84
Place Dauphine, 36, 39
Place de la Concorde, 18
Place de l'Opéra, 59
Place des Vosges, 55, 58
Place du Tertre, 110, 111, 112
Place Louis Lépine, 44
Place Pigalle, 17, 111
Place Vauban, 14
Pont de la Tournelle, 33
Pont Neuf, 36, 39, 42
Porte de Vanves, 20
Poulbot, 112
Prévert, Jacques, 71, 108
Proust, 51

Quai aux Fleurs, 44
Quai d'Anjou, 33
Quai de Béthune, 33
Quai de Conte, 39
Quai d'Orsay, 16

Rabelais, 55
Rachel, 51
Racing Club de Paris, the, 79
Restaurant aux Gourmets, 26
Restaurant Paul, 36
Restaurant Véfour, 108
Richelieu, Cardinal, 55
Rocca, Robert, 85
Rodin, 14
Rodin, Musée, 14
Rotonde, the (café), 80
Rue Chaptal, 96
Rue de Beaujolais, 108
Rue de Furstenberg, 66
Rue de Montpensier, 108
Rue de la Charbonnière, 99
Rue de la Gaîté, 81
Rue de Rennes, 71
Rue de Rivoli, 58
Rue des Beaux-Arts, 65
Rue des Francs-Bourgeois, 58
Rue des Rosiers, 87
Rue de Sévigné, 55
Rue de Valois, 108
Rue de Varenne, 14
Rue Drouot, 94
Rue Jacob, 87
Rue Lepic, 110, 111
Rue Mouffetard, 83
Rue Notre Dame de Lorette, 85
Rue Saint-Antoine, 55
Rue Saint-Dominique, 14, 114
Rue St.-Louis-en-l'Ile, 33

Sacré-Coeur, le, 102, 111
Saint Sulpice, Church of, 66
St. Germain-des-Prés, 80
St. Germain-des-Prés, Church of, 65
St. Paul-St. Louis, Church of, 55
Sand, George, 53
Sartre, Jean-Paul, 63, 70, 71
Seine, the, 61, 111
Sièges de la Ville, the, 58
Silence Antenne, 76
Souplex, Raymond, 86
Square du Vert-Galant, 39
Théâtre Bobino, 81
Théâtre du Palais-Royal, 108

Théâtre du Grand Guignol, 96
Tribunal de Commerce, 44
Trocadéro, Square du, 79
Tuileries Gardens, 19

Verlaine, Paul, 54
'*Vespasiennes, les*', 16
Villon, François, 47
Voltaire, 34, 47

Watteau, 54
Wilde, Oscar, 51, 65

Zola, Emile, 54, 75